Titles

Oh To Tell the Story, Chronicles of an
Afro-American Woman
Poetic expressions

This Way to Sunny, Love poems

Cynthia Sherrell

Gemini Diaries
heart of a woman

Made in the United States of America November 2013

Cover design by Cynthia Sherrell
Photography contribution by Your Endless Moments Photography

Table of contents

Majoring the minor

My weary soul wondered when change was coming,
my heart never faltered, it just kept on humming,
a song of victory, even though defeat seemed near,
my heart opened itself to grip God's message and hear,
direction on the best route to take,
and what decisions to make.

Being here, somewhere I had never been before
was scary and surreal by far,
walking blindly, feeling my way through,
trusting God is by my side helping me to,
the place He'd promised many decades ago,
a place requiring total submission and growth.

At many points I wanted to turn and run
I'd cry in the corner wondering what I could have done
why was I being so resistant
why must my heart be so hesitant
though God said I'd never be forsaken or left
clinging to what was familiar was my safety net.

I'd sit and listen to songs of glory
so they could push me through my story
to be shared with the world at large
one of fierce faith and taking charge
of the destiny promised before my birth
a life I agreed to before entering earth.

Along the path came a few bright stars
people who helped me to remember my strengths
people who prayed for me continually,
loved me unconditionally, and
encouraged me to keep moving forward.

I love these angels and thank God immensely
for allowing these special individuals to find me
seems like their timing was perfect indeed
because they came when I was in a pivotal place secretly
they helped me to overcome, come through and see clearly
the path of victory God paved for me.

Sunrise

Support listened to me not make sense,
while I sifted through unrehearsed thoughts;
support told me the truth,
when I only wanted to see things my way;
demanded nothing of me
but that I be myself.

Support slept on my couch last night
while I slept in my bed;
hugged me this morning,
then left without asking for anything in return.

And by this you shall know

Rebirths every day,
new revelations in every way,
purified reflections of a brighter way,
peaceful release to useless pain that wants to stay,
this is how you know you're living.

10:22am

Can't believe it had been a year
since she's been here
my heart. weary and torn
my prayer hopeful yet worn
on one hand I wanted her to stay on earth with me
on the other, I wanted her in heaven flying free
I told God some time ago
that when it was her time to go
by phone, I didn't want to know

It was bright and early Saturday morning
my phone rang; it was my aunt asking
if my grandmother I'd be joining
I said yes actually I am on my way
a cool breeze floated through the air sitting on my window bay
the thought never crossed my mind
that this would be the last time
I would see my grandmother alive.

Entering the room I examined her body
I looked at the woman that prayed and protected me
looking down remembering special days shared
all the secrets I bared
and how she kept each one
remembering years of fun.
Looking at her hands, recalling shared recipes,
thinking about Sunday mornings at church,
when she would sing beautifully without having to rehearse.
Before taking my seat
I grabbed her hand and kissed her cheek

Whispering softly in her ear how I loved her so
granting her permission to go
thanking her for being a wonderful grandmother
she waved at someone, I think it was her deceased brother
I rubbed her hair and the side of her face,
softly sang Amazing Grace
tears started streaming down my face
I felt loving angels fill the place.

Shortly afterwards my aunt entered the room
my grandfather followed her very soon
grandmamma waved at him, his reply was "Hi"
he walked out of the room not knowing she was actually
saying goodbye
grandmamma began taking her last few breaths
as badly as I wanted her to stay
lovingly supporting her in death
singing her favorite hymns assuring her we'd be fine
and would see her in due time,
Jesus was now calling her home,
tears streamed as I said, it's okay to go be with him
She departed this life at 10:22am

Rivers of light

I almost slipped,
my foot almost gave
longing for love for as long as I could remember
in the arms of my mother
a teen, confused, left alone to bear the journey
of parenthood on her own.
I looked for love in between sheets
of mean and callous streets
on cloud nine.
I searched for a concubine
countless nights of roaming the lost
dark places of the world
this little girl
still with me
loving to be free.
I couldn't find love in matrimony
was something wrong with me?
Was my heart stony,
was I made for love,
was I made to love?
Broken, I pretended
my pain had been mended
but it was lie
everything I believed was a lie.

I press

Gotta go on anyhow
even though I feel let down
even though I feel alone
gotta go on anyhow
my help feels weak
my ambition is meek
but I gotta go on anyhow.
I cry more than I smile
I can't locate my sense of style
but I gotta go on anyhow
I forgot my purpose,
lost my vision
my life has no rhythm
with limited precision
but I gotta go on anyhow.
They say, stand still and see the hand of the Lord
stand still and know he is God
I know in my heart who he is
and that he lives inside of me
that's how I keep going on anyhow.

Burning trees

The woods are coming, the woods are coming
from the window their hatred can be seen
the first settlers, made strangers to their own land,
their home land
the woods are here with an army weak, yet long
justifying this indignation by any means necessary
what give these savages the right to earth and sky
take their land, kill them, their families, they all must die
the woods assassinated equality
like strange fruit and hung it from oak trees
beat back the fight and stripped hope from the masses
then lied saying Jesus was white
I hate this America! I hate the breath that I breathe!
This land of the bound, home of the lost
let's massacre the woods,
chop down their trees of injustice, burn their cynical reproach
invade their land and steal all they've worked for
remove these despised little peasants from civil society
they have no civility, this embedded by their forefathers
a wicked generation, a prideful nation.
Mercy? No
This America is not yours or ours,
the woods of America are filled with fruitless trees
The soil of this America, enriched with sacrificial blood
I hate this America! I hate the breath that I breathe!

Spirited touch

We collect ourselves, bottling pained yesterdays
severed hearts, trying to appear normal
broken limbs and bleeding souls desiring to be healed
with decomposed hope concealed,
but I see through
I see you,
looking into your longings to be coaxed, mended and spared
your wall came tumbling down
the night we slept in each other's arms
night visions revealed the content of your character, bringing
me into the fold
reaching out to you and simultaneously trying to hold
your burdens, desiring to free your soul.
A childlike manner disguised as one liberated and glee
private squanders of defeat arrested your ambition
so cowardly
you wander,
wondering when will someone rescue thee
when will someone rescue thee from thyself,
and from the silent death
you die every day
Once more
I reached for you while the door
of your heart was slightly ajar
your hand you lifted,
but your mind drifted,
back to when it hurt to love and trust in another
stumbling back to the known,
the brigade of fear wrestled with you blowing,
the possibility of newness.
so in the distance waved I, smiling and thanking
God for this brief moment in time with you,

Spirited touch (continued)

You taught me things anew
trust what I hear, know my limits, and
not to force something to be when nothings in it.
You are a treasured soul and a valued man
I pray thine gifts would flourish within thine hands
I pray your heart's desires would always be granted
and that the love of your woman would never be slanted,
in the distance wave I, smiling and thanking
God for this brief moment in time.

Woman I saw

A thick white woman,
red and black hair,
bout a size twelve
a rubber band holds her medium length hair in a ponytail,
carrying six movies she sits at the computer checking
her Face book page
slumped in the chair, wearing unhappiness fresh
moving the falling strand of hair from her face
she turns around as if she feels my eyes upon her.

Goodbye

When we first met, I had no interest in you
yes you were nice looking, tall, athletic build with nice eyes
too
but I was in a peaceful place in life with no intentions of
building something new
but overtime, your persistence changed my view

When I think this whole thing over, I wish I wouldn't have
changed my mind
I wrestled over and over if I was being blind
blinded by your conversation, something you rarely find
a professional and intellectual man, one of a kind

Now here we are, as distant and two can be
how we got here, I don't know, I only followed the signals
you sent to me,
but I'm ok with saying goodbye and us walking free
because I know nothing will ever evolve between you and me

I bid you farewell and pray you have a good life
a peaceful pardon, there's no strife
I hope you find a loving and supportive wife
one whose love showers you rife

I pray your business does well
that your customers go and tell
others about the swell
job you do, and many items you'd sell

Goodbye

Making love

Panting heavily
he on top of me
the man of my dreams
my husband and faithful friend
my ride or die until the end
picturing my life without him
days without his kisses
or passionate hugs
lying next to him, knowing
he'll be there in the middle of the night
to hold me tight.
Life without him, an awful sight
in the heat of the night, I yell Papi
but not in a fatherly way
he protects me and take care of my needs
he cried at the unbirth of our seeds
he opens his heart to learn a new way
and blesses the day
I became his Mrs.
this man here, my hubby
shows no mercy when loving
me, or pleasuring my body
he is tall, dark and sexy
the man right for me
as I lie beneath him
wetting my joy stick
his moans and thrashings
cause me to open more than my heart
imperfectly perfect for me
beads of sweat fall from his body
as he pant heavily
on top of me
he pulls me close

Making love (continued)

telling me how much he loves me
and how taking my love away would hurt him
we laugh at each other and have fun alone
when we are a part I can't wait to get home
a troubled past wears at his mind
I look in his eyes
pull him close to me,
say a prayer for him, silently.
It's his time now to experience joy
and let the little boy
inside of him be free
he pants heavily
while on top of me
I love him more with each stroke
can't imagine being the cause
of his heart being broke
anticipating this love for so long
one able to endure life
and stand strong
one where I could unapologetically be me
and embrace another wholeheartedly
one that God joined together
every time I see him my heart leaps
I feel like an adolescent girl
in a fantasy world
somebody pinch me so I can wake
ouch, this is not a dream
but as delicious as butter pecan ice cream
I look up to him and kiss his chin
he smiles tenderly at me, I grin
my heart jumps at the passion in his eyes

Making love (continued)

and the throbbing between my thighs
his eyes hold mine hostage
as he hits that spot
slow grinding his thrusts go deep
I talk dirty to him
he licks his lips
I grab his hips
and bite my bottom lip
his nipples get hard
I kiss his chest and tease his nipples
his stokes becomes steady and strong
sending ripples
through my body
Moaning, I lick my lips
I talk dirty, he strokes harder
I moan louder, he strokes harder
I lick my breasts, he strokes harder
he strokes harder panting heavily
I love this man on top of me

Mirror, mirror

I am beautiful
I am beautiful can't you see
from the soul in my head
to the pride of my stride
I am beautiful

Mirror, mirror
tell me your version
reveal to me
your mystical resolves,
you know all my secrets
and have witnessed the conversion
of a dismayed teen
with low self-esteem
to a woman caught in between
her future and her past
to now a beautiful queen

Through the years I've stood before you
sad, confused
lonely, with the blues
but you, mirror
you never let me forget
I was beautiful

No matter my appearance saggy eyes, crusty or red
crazy or lazy hair, the before and after
your uncompromised truths became my real love
when I looked at you I saw beauty

Mirror, mirror (continued)

The image you shared caused me to rethink the matter
and forsake the negative chatter
going on inside my head
the picture they painted
hindered my ability to get acquainted
with the reflection I'd see
when you looked back at me

Mirror, mirror
the place where love was birthed
the place where I could be free
cause you were the only one looking back at me
and the picture I'd see pure beauty

Now one with your truths,
surrendered I my worldview
your affirmations became my hallelujah salvation
oh yes I've been redeemed
I am a beautiful queen
I am beautiful
I am beautiful can't you see

Dreams

Illuminated answers, a starry night,
a guiding light,
dreams, deliverance to a wondering slave
Black Moses in a sense
explaining compounds and elements

Mother nature's heart for me,
condensing confusion
dreams like an early morning sunrise
awaken and infuse wisdom
shortening my fall

Whispers glaze my soul while lying still,
looking up to heaven, baby blue skies
chant lullabies
as wispy billows travel by
in slow motion,
dreams like ocean waves
chaos and conflict,
money found in open places
tell a powerful story, the matters of my heart.

Ask me tomorrow

I'm bloated,
my vigor for life has floated,
the sensible me, coated
with a hard shell

My aggravation,
and patience have
both reached their limitation
this head pounding frustration
makes me want to yell.

No one is favored,
no moment is savored

I am uncomfortable and confused
and hating this ugly blues

Same sex lover

I'm inspired to love you
the respect we have for one another
is a glue
that holds this bond together
through thick and thin
sunshine and rain
no matter the weather
I'm inspired to love you

People look at you and instantaneously
they see a dike and strike
the thought of getting to know,
the you I know.
Judgment they pass exposing discrimination.

Is there really a solution
to this illusion?
Like really,
how can people take a poll
and choose where your soul
will rest eternally?

I mean really are they there
when you go before your Master
and your sins and grieves are bare?
What's the deal
are people for real?
what cross did they die upon
what length of love have they gone
to love you brotherly
the commandment Christ echoes constantly.

Same sex lover (continued)

I say, forget them whomever they be
and walk liberally
in who you are
cause the truth is
we all have sinned
some have aborted kids,
scrutiny they can't take
so they keep their truths hid.

I'm inspired to love you
we ride and die tight
for when life bring contrite
emotions, sadness and pain
let my love be the push you need to reign.

Behind the waterfall

Behind the waterfall lies a compass to pain,
behind the waterfall songs of affliction slain;
behind the waterfall a fatherless son ponders,
behind the waterfall a battered mind wonders;
behind the waterfall a vexed heart thirst,
behind the waterfall a mother hears the worst;
behind the waterfall an opposed lad of war speaks,
behind the waterfall an abandoned child seeks;
behind the waterfall are generations of civil rights,
behind the waterfall a failing student fights;
behind the waterfall a maniacal vagabond pinched by misery,
behind the waterfall loathes a lesbian segregated by sexuality;
behind the waterfall disappears a love sick heart,
behind the waterfall a molestation victim incurs a new start;
behind the waterfall wails a child laying their mother to rest,
behind the waterfall curses the wife of a drunken pest;
behind the waterfall cries a sullen soul,
behind the waterfall mourns a distressed widow.

The phone is ringing

I don't want to talk
I don't want to listen
I don't want to explain
I don't want to complain
I don't want to understand
I don't want to be a friend
I don't want to pretend
I don't want to comprehend
I don't want to lie
I don't want to cry
I don't want to agree
I don't want you trying to make sense of me
I don't want to hurt
I don't want to be rude or curt
I don't want to analyze
I don't want to compromise
I don't want to act concerned
I don't want to wait my turn
I don't want to answer the phone

Women only

A place of uncertainty,
a space where I'm unsure of me
and question my abilities.
I'm trying to remember how I broke free
the last times
the last times?
Yeah, the last times,
when lust broke covenants
leaving me to deal with the remnants
of having to piece back together my womanhood,
having to leave childhood dreams of being his one true love
baring his children and making a stable home
dreams turned into aching realities
cause he shook my stability,
I didn't have a plan B,
I didn't plan on him cheating
crying last oh but so long
finding strength to be strong and move on
I was uncertain of my ability
to survive the road up ahead, so I stalled, and stalled until I
couldn't stall anymore.
I ran into another, six years my senior
his agenda appeared to be to love me,
the closer I got I could see he wasn't right for me
making this clear was challenging
he didn't want to let go,
my need for stability caused me to stay
something unbeautiful was conceived
now I deal with choices, choices, choices
these voices, I can't rid these freaking voices
lying on the table propping my legs, begging God to forgive
and forget this sin

Women only (continued)

I look at her and say, "Can I see it"?
Her dry reply, "You don't want to see this".
A part of me died that would never be resurrected
breathing like the best of them
my secrets go undetected
one step, one step after the other
gets me closer to being able to recover

Home again

Witnessing the transition from night to day
metaphorically mirrored my present state
the clear moon and quiet wind of souls moving on
symbolized the day's long
oh how I wish I was home again

Like fire

You laugh wittingly, telling me not to worry
besides what's the point of worrying, or thinking too hard
the truth you are seeking is already here
the light within is damaged and dimly shine forth
breaking free from the matrimony of bondage
is my heart's desire,
seems like no matter how hard I pray
or how fervently I lay
down these burdens, they are my life sentence,
the cross was begrudgingly assigned to me long before I came
into existence
imaginative lies
they say I contrive
but I know what the truth is
I traced my genealogy
and found adultery
murder, mayhem, and misery followed me here
assassinating my future and ridiculing my sanity
this air is dirty,
the musty foul stench of oppression offends my nostrils
feel like a stranger in my own land.

Digging him

Brand new
my feelings for you
thought through
my feelings so true
who knew
I had no clue
when my feelings grew
but I'm so digging you
now tell me what's your view.

Save us Lord

Remembering summer days when love fervently burned
night sweats, lightning bugs and cool lemonade
on grandmama's porch, a place where bitterness churned
like the lemon rind
floating to the top of my glass
where beatings and curse words shoved us
right to the front pew of grandpappy's church
night sweats and offering plates with choir selections
powdered lies sprinkle the chancel like April showers
who are marked by death through demonic powers.

Black Moses

Bound, enslaved, yoked
trapped, pained, choked
poor, angry, thralled
settled, bitter, stalled
packing, following, hearing,
moving, singing, fearing,
cold, wet, hungry, weary
stumbling, unsure, anxious, bleary
close, encouraged, visioning
assured, positive, positioning
there, free, emancipated
tired, free, liberated
reminiscing, smiling, crying
new, peaceful, flying

Let's stand together

What is this fight you have conjured in your mind?
Haven't I taught you anything over this span of time?
I am tired of this fight of deception
I am tired of this fight that began with your conception.
there's nothing to defend
let's stop playing games and lose the pretend
a divided house can't stand strong
before too long
it will fall, it will fail.
We can't go on this way
I call a truce hoping you will follow
hoping you will humble your heart
and agree to stay
in love, full and free
besides it's so tiring
to keep up this anguish and hostility
can't we just be one big happy family?
Do you have to point out all my imperfections
and make corrections
on everything I do?
Must you judge my every action
and cut my kinds deeds into fractions?
I have loved you since you were formed
I vowed to protect you from hurt and harm
but now it just seems like that is not enough for you
the only thing I know to do is pray,
pray for your stony heart
pray for a fresh start
pray for a mind renewed
pray you'll release the need to reprove.

We can be a big loving family,
just accept me for who I am as I have thee.

Gentle beauty

Young, brave hearted soul,
this tumultuous world,
a spectacle to humanity
revering neither the suckling babe
nor the sagaciously old
a bitterly cold land, that
attempted to assassin the gentle beauty you are
tenderly young,
gracefully tenacious
soft child facing the wind
clothed with temperance
this in remembrance
of you, a queen
destined to be
a messenger of the heart,
a messenger admired by the commoners,
a welcoming light for this mourning world

Rhapsody

Be still my child, sit and let me free your mind,
I am day, new and whole, a chance to bud and blossom
I am day, purely a hopeful canvas, begging for your creativity
Be still, relax with me, lie down in the warmth of promise
I am day, savor this smidgen of valor
I am day, dance with me, feel my pulse, pace thine heart

Be quiet my child, hush the weary issues inside thine soul
I am day, close your eyes and dream with me
I am day, study newness bringeth and relish in my fortitude
Be quiet my child, hold your peace and find strength
I am day, a journey awaiting exploration
I am day, a solitary fable desiring for thine.

Still waters

Fresh rain, a cry in the night
flesh pain, a sigh in the fight

The storm brewed since youth
the harm chewed wince truth

rippled reflections try her fate
crippled perfections dry her gait

The view of hope wake her heart
the hue of cope shake her start

Poetry power

My only friend, my pen
new sheets collect my thoughts judging me not.
Complete, whole and healed am I
knowing my inner musings are sealed
only revealed
by choice.

My passionate voice
carries a message of hope,
a message of strength,
a message of compassion
speaking life to dying souls and half beating hearts
a blank canvas is where healing starts.

Poor choices

I lost my focus for a moment
my kind heart was mistaken to be weak
but thank God for constantly
keeping his hand of protection over me
people come in the name of purity
but really their motives are not right
I lost my focus for a moment
but I thank God for restoring my sight.

"Holiness had left the place."
Scattered sheep

Scattered sheep

E'vr since he was a lil boy
he dreamt of pastoring his own flock
it wasn't far-fetched, it was built in his stock
his father, a pastor though of not many
was more concerned about dollars than a penny.

As he grew he always knew
having his own church was his calling,
nothing and no one would keep him stalling
even though his pastor said it was not time
he took his family with a made up mind
starting out with only a few
he preached his heart out as though thousands were in the pew
he summoned his kids and grandkids to follow his dream
no matter how ill-prepared he seemed
his family became the church choir
so things would not get dire
he asked his in-laws and siblings to join
promising them extra coins.

Others came in from churches near and far
when members from the Kendal family came,
there was a silent war.
The head of the Kendal family had dirt on the pastor
he soon became head of the deacon board faster
than others thought
but the pastor could be bought
to keep his secrets.

Before long rumors, started to spread
that the pastor had a mistress in his bed
his siblings and in-laws wouldn't stand the mess
they packed their things and decided to jet

Scattered sheep (continued)

The first lady embarrassed and demeaned
tucked her emotions away but they were tearing at the seams.

To take the heat away from his life was his desire
the pastor set the whole church on fire
se scraped up the insurance funds and remained
but things were no longer the same

He treated others better than his family
often causing them pain openly
making hurtful remarks over the pulpit
he was a "throw the rock and hide your hands" culprit.

The insurance company caught wind of his scheme
after the second fire and attempt to try and smooth things
he was now on the fraud list
and his congregation got wind of it
they felt, something was just not right
they began to question his motives and whereabouts at night

The ministers formed an alliance and began to take a stand
they prayerfully confronted the man
they looked up to and honored every year
begging for the truth through every tear
the pastor cowardly looked away
noticing a snake in the office window bay
he knew he had been exposed
but his pride would not allow him to let go
he pleaded for the men's forgiveness and reconcile
the church was moving to a new building
and he needed them to stay awhile

Scattered sheep (continued)

Shortly after the move it was only a matter of time
before the congregation began to decline
those that remained
were either glory stealers, mentally challenged or couldn't be
contained
holiness had left the place,
a dark cloud hovered over the space
neither prayer nor fasting could break the demonic hold
or undo the satanic mold
that had settled in.

The first lady's health began to go down
the news spread quickly around town
she had spent many years in a dead-end matrimony
and was ready to meet Jesus in a blessed homecoming
the pastor lied to the church saying she wanted time alone
he lied to the first lady saying the church said they'll see her
when she come home.

She never returned to the feeble four walls
the congregation was hurt most of all
they desired to be there for the woman who had prayed for
their souls
she was gone now and would never be told
how much they loved her and missed her so
why their pastor lied, they'd never know
their first lady rested in a peaceful sleep
thus began the process of scattered sheep
going here and there
nearly everywhere
families clashed and went separate ways
some found other churches, many became strays.

Anticipating love

Fervently sought thee, love
almost caught thee, love
I slightly remember the feel of you
think I was about two sitting on the lap of my mother
not again until age of four
when I walked through the door,
to love his tears away.

Waiting on the porch anticipating love's return
calmness of spirit, watching full moons
slumber came all too soon
but love never came.

I say to myself
love will come and stay awhile
I use to trust make believe stories
fantastical promises of love worthwhile
new dawns and decades later
it's hard to know
if love will ever show.

After the age of four
the next time love knocked on my door
was at the birth of my seed
funny, I didn't feel love when she was being conceived
at least I know love is real
but the kind of love I want to feel
is shared by two who become one
and can't be undone
when life seems unbearable
hopefully before the end of my days
and my home become the grave
love will come.

Rainstorm

Looking out the window, the wonder of God
befuddled me, clapping raindrops
praised Jehovah
boisterous thunder, emulating the voice of God
commanded authority,
silenced poignant conversations of day to day life.

Not if, but when

It's sad to see
this is your reality
but I too can understand
how you my man
have gotten to this place

It's painful
to constantly be hurt
folks talking to you crazy
and running your feelings in the dirt.

You see, I know this pain all too well
but there's a few things I must sell
"When you go looking for let downs that's what you find"
and all wounds can be healed through love and time".

It's comfortable to be content in your reality
in your reserved space
you're able to move at your own pace, but
we were created to love
to give and receive it
just chose to believe it
and your dreams will come true.

Gathering leaves

Will the day ever come
will the moment ever exist
when I am able to resist
fear, its grip
challenges my faith and strips
my ambition.

Will the time ever be seen
when I will conquer the mean
heartless feeling of defeat.

Will the hour come to pass
when I can lose myself
in and through myself
where at last I am free.

If the hour ever came where fear was tamed
faith would devour my enemies
and let me go free,
second guessing and
constant digressing
would lose its power.

In that moment
life would be joyous,
smiles, happiness
and love would unselfishly
open up to me

Looking free, living bound

Can I pour my heart out to you,
will you listen to me,
promise not to judge me the way the preacher man do.
See I have always thought I was ugly, stupid and wouldn't
amount to much
I didn't have a lot growing up,
my daddy left and I had a hard time dealing with it.
I didn't pay attention in school cause all I could think about
was the bully waiting to beat me up.
I didn't feel sexy or think of sex as pleasurable
I was molested and was told to shut up.
See I do want to express my feelings
or let you know I like you a lot
I feel unworthy of love more often than not
I know I send mixed signals and I'm hard to read
I really try hard not to be
I cry a lot because the yoke of my past grips me tight
and when I'm lying in my bed at night
I ask God why did I have to be born
why do I have to be scarred.
I cry because I have to teach my daughter's how to live free
but truth is I think of dying every day,
I was defeated before I came from my mother's womb
I just want to know you won't bail on me because I'm
entombed
but I understand, who wants to love the walking dead
who can love a woman that can't escape the thoughts of
bondage in her head
I am lovable at least I hope to be
I know I act like I don't want you getting close to me
but it's unintentional, I want you close all the time
I just feel like my birth was an unjust crime
I wish you could be patient with me and see my heart
I wish you could see past all the barriers I put up and chose me
to embark
but hell I know you got problems, issues and feelings too
just wanted to pour my heart out to you

34 seconds to anywhere

Take your time
ye panting heart
gleeful and full of possibilities.

Open your eyes
see the welcoming arms of a
spiteful nation
one that's ready to sift you
refine your dreams, and
bake your fears.

Go hither
plant your seeds of good works
for on the banks of heaven
your reward awaits.

Smile ever so brightly
for when night falls
no man will see or hear
the noble works you imparted

Fragile heart

For far too long
believing life had to be hard was my song
it was hard to see life in a happy way
because of this, I dreaded seeing most days
it was easier to believe men were dogs
and lazy as logs
going so far to believe all men lied
they were emotionless, and never cried
life mirrored my beliefs
offering no relief
until one day my spirit guides spoke through my dreams
showing my life tearing at the seams
my world as I knew was crumbling before my eyes
it was time to release the lies
I had believed throughout my years
and embrace a new way of being minus the fears.
I use to believe there was never enough money to spare
let alone share
I agreed, secretly in my heart
that money didn't want any part
of my life
when I became a wife
it was hard to understand
him as a man
it was hard to receive
that the things I believed
was going to ruin
our union.
I was willing to change but didn't know where to start
so I went back to praying from my heart
I told God my life needed to go in a different direction,
I repented for constantly second guessing
the divine plan

Fragile heart (continued)

I thanked God for the man
he placed as my head,
asked for forgiveness for the things I'd said
things that spoke death to our circumstance
I fervently asked for a second chance.
God embraced me and charged me to trust him
he told me I was loved and His precious gem
he gave me a word in the scriptures
instructing I walk by faith using mental pictures
Psalms 1, God promised prosperity
as long as I kept his word faithfully
God understood how my life got turned around
and offered his love to keep me safe and sound.

Marked for death

A fat little girl
just like her mother,
her mother teaches her nothing
about living, eating or being a woman
she eats while lying in bed
she eats when playing the Wii
she is a fat little girl
and fits in well
with the other fat people in the world
it's sad though
because she is only ten
and is the size of someone
twice her age
is she marked for death?
Diabetes, high blood pressure, heart disease
with the way she eats and lays around
she is bound to have one of these.
Fried chicken, chips, junk,
she eats daily
no exercise, no fruit unless canned
this little girl is fat, I think she's damned.

My King

I dreamt of him
a king, my king
he did exist
his attributes completed my list
my king, tall, nice build and clean cut
my personal admirer, intrigued by my strut
a job, his own place and car
a humble man, no superstar
has to love kids and even have a couple of his own,
a charming smile
his mind flexible and strong
My king.

A Gemini's diary

When I look out to life I see a never ending river,
a book of blank pages
a mystery in mind but it doesn't have to be
because I can write the story's ending
the story to tell my daughter's daughter's daughter.
When I awake, a blank script awaits
sometimes like a nagging gnat bothering me,
guidance I seek, seems like
being told is easier than figuring it out
but I am the author of this book, the director of this play
like David I pray
Lord teach my hands to war
teach me how to win this never ending battle
teach me who, what, where, how and when
oh and why, knowing why is essential to where
this never ending river leads and how the story reads
a mystery that doesn't have to be.
This journey brings comrades, summon angels to
give me a sign, go before me, and tell me the report.

Reunion

And then there was you
who made me laugh
when I wanted to cry
who talked me down
when I wanted to die
who told me the truth
when I wanted a lie
who held my hand
when I was shy
you were the light
that restored my sight
my angel, you

Secrets

Sitting here thinking, wondering if the thoughts playing
over and over in my head could be heard
here it was the third,
and last time I would suffer this way.
When I woke up this morning
I declared this would be the only day
of my life I would take this path,
like the other woman here, we held wrath in our womb,
judgment and condemnation grew there too
the women's only club, a place cold and numb
looking at each other wondering her story
pondering how she would do after the glory
is sapped from her body,
well at least that's what I was thinking
as I sat there sinking
deeper into caves of depression.
I felt alone in a crowded room.
They called my name, my knees felt weak
Slowly rising, walking towards the front humble and meek
Had she did this before
does she think I'm a whore
has she sent me to hell
do she think I should be locked under the jail,
these thoughts and more
rushed my head while pacing the floor.
She led me to a quiet room, there a notebook
others before me barred their souls
I hesitated before writing
a short brief note,
"May God give you peace in your heart and mind,
may you forgive yourself for this moment in time.
Quietly undressing to lie on the table
questioning if I was able
to go through with this deed
of aborting my seed
crying reminding myself this was best
after sighing a heavy breath I finished getting undressed

Rolling like thunder

A spy to injustice, sitting at the foot of humanitarianism
myself, a giant like those who've gone before me
their path boisterous, freedom writers, they lived the truth.

She nursed the ill back to health
lead legions free, Moses in her own right
a determined soul who sought the way
a liberated light, a secret negro spiritual
ringing in the hearts of the free
a giant who walked worthily
a giant was she.

Two decades of bondage before fleeing to the wonder city
a creative scriber after the heart of his people
a mixed breed, conductor on the ride to glory
literary art birthed through his loins
eloquent in speech, rhetorically appropriate for the times
a giant in his prime
a giant not afraid to climb.

Believing shining mountain tops, with
a sanctuary of fruitful trees in the valley below
a young soldier in the midst of the war
with undeterred faith justice would come

Silly girl

I think I played myself when I let you in
I think I played myself when we moved past friends
I think I played myself when I said let's spend more time
I think I played myself when I thought you wanted to be mine
I think I played myself when I heard something you didn't say
I think I played myself by not looking the other way

Teens

Shame them, leave em on their knees
cause really they don't understand the fight
nor have the right
to be so doggone defensive
if I could, I would smack her
smack some sense in that young brain
cause see she don't know a doggone thing
nothing about learning, loving or living

His words

Words move me
with melodies and beats,
with passion between the sheets
they soothe me
eating dinner
with my winner
words and his soft glance
words comfort my heart, they speak life
not just any words, but his words

Autumn blues

When we first met I knew we wouldn't remain
yet I went along with what you wanted
all the while holding tightly to the inability
to get close to you
no matter how hard I tried
there was always uneasiness tugging at the piece of possibility
and now like the red tip of a lit match, you're gone
the time we've spent together, the conversations we've shared,
the laughs we've exchanged
are mere afterthoughts engraved into yesterday, buried forever
the residue of disappointment line the crevices of my heart
saying goodbye pains me, so
I limit welcoming arms to control waving hands
saying goodbye pains me, so
I limit thoughts of what could have been to control thoughts of
what is
saying goodbye pains me, so
I limit my hellos to control my goodbyes

The beach

The rain washes the seaboard as the tide hits the bank
resemblance of sovereignty dissolved
the waves rush my thoughts

Special moment

Lying next to you, being with you
the other night
felt right
in every way
opening up, letting you in,
the softness of your skin,
the tenderness of your stroke
passionately broke
through aged barriers
ones that made living scarier
than it needed to be.
Your stiff serenaded muted places
as waterfalls cascaded
I couldn't help calling your name
you felt so good
our bodies in sync
speaking a language we both understood.
Looking at the place,
the sacred space
where time stood still
where we denied not ourselves the need to feel
the warmth of the moment, we glanced at romance,
affection deepened our connection,
desire took us higher, being free produced true intimacy,
Lying next to you, being with you
the other night
felt oh so right
in every way

Identity crisis

Each step I took felt like a dreaded nightmare
how did I get here
I use to be on top of the world
a once simple and lonely girl
now a vibrant sexy woman in her own class
independent, smart with a career moving fast
two cars, a townhome and money in the bank
my life was great, I was a long way from Dank
who is Dank, that was me in my teens
trying to fit in while being stuck between
low self-esteem and barely any clothes, back then
I wanted to disappear and be the girl no one chose
life was hard during those years
overweight and ugly, my nights were filled with tears
but here I was now, a wholesome women with men to choose
determined to never be in a position where I'd lose
but now as I walk this starry dark night
with tears flowing, I wondered why things were tight
money was scarce, I had no job and in a smaller house
life was supposed to be cheery, I even had a new spouse
but here I was losing all that I had built
every day I woke up to unsettled guilt
who am I and what am I doing with my life
I have my own business,
have written books but unhappiness was rife
feeling like a failure in my daughter's eyes
this cool fall night I wanted to know
what to do with my life and which way to go
questioning if my crumbling life was because I got married
or due to the ambiguity I carried
once driven, full of zeal and heart
now here I was feeling lost not knowing where to start

Pure no more

Should I just slap her and get it over with
staying angry and being mean takes so much energy
should I just cry and let out my pain
what satisfaction comes from my cruelty to her
really, excessive punishments and growling will not replace
what she gave away,
it will not bring back what she lost

I've talked before, long and longer
but somehow she missed the bottom line
this time, though, she crossed the line
the sight of her angers me
her longing for me to look her in the eyes angers me
her non apologetic demeanor pisses me off

How long will this last I wonder
I don't know, but I do know
she hurt me badly this time and I'm not ready to let it go

Thank you

You were there at a time when I needed you most
putting your life on hold when my heart was pain's host,
my grandmother had died
even though we were divorced, you listened when I cried
you offered words of inspiration and care
even said a prayer to lighten my despair
you kept the kids a few extra days
and offered to come over and help in immeasurable ways.
I don't think I ever told you how much your deeds meant
I don't think I ever said thank you for caring about me
during this painful event.

Even though we had divorced and went on with our life
you were nice to me even though I was no longer your wife.
No one is taught how to be a part, we just learn by default
we sit through court hearings that capture blame and fault
often times we give little time to let our hearts heal
we keep moving on, pushing down a pain that's real.

When my grandmother died, I was lost and hurt
I didn't want to see her lowered in the dirt
I didn't want to wake up to tomorrow without her here
I didn't want to accept she was no longer near.

When my grandmother died, a part of me died too
your thoughtfulness and kind deeds helped me make it
through. Thank you.

Possibilities' peak

Seems like it's the same ole thing
love longing to be found
yet remaining lost forever
hearts filled with possibilities
and desired realities
seem to never surface.

I'd be lying if I said I felt no connection to you
as you held me under the rain, or
when our lips pressed hope closely to the edge, or
that night our bodies blended
arousing a future between the two of us.

I'd be lying if I said I don't think of you often
wondering what you're doing or
how your day was.

My heart is tired of anticipation,
tired of being happiness' joke,
I choke on these words now
will love ever come?

Sun up moon down

Can we really recreate the moment,
that moment when we indulged
leaving the memory of judgment
wandering in the wind.
If we repeat that night
taking delight
in sinful pleasures
hugging and undressing
kissing and caressing
moaning and expressing,
will we leave our minds wondrously guessing?

For my heart's desire is to date you
then mate you not to merely sex you
and occasionally text you.

To share a spirited touch, a celestial encounter
where the story of our souls
are revealed through the windows of our being,
then at sunrise the tenderness of euphoria
politely wraps herself around us.

For during twilight's existence
the passage way to my essence opened, and
the strength of your manliness tastefully explored
God's intellect, his demonstrated love for mankind, and
movements in the moment unite our wandering souls.
Redoing what has already been done
will be more than physical gratification
but a budding formation,
a purified creation,
a quiet journey we'll have just begun.

Giving up

I have so much love to give but it seems as though
the kind of love I have to offer is not really valued
I mean, my daughters they profit from and appreciate it
but they were designed to love me unconditionally
all who enter my life enter a special place in my heart
because they are God's children and because I love him so.
I reverence his children and see him in them
treating them civilly, giving to the needing
and sacrifice for the poor.
My love seems valueless can't seem to ascend to love
in the heart of a man,
who will love me as Christ loves the church
I dreamt that one day it will happen
the longer I live, the more I see that day never coming
I'm so sick in my heart.
Sick and disgusted with disappointment
for my entire life,
all I ever wanted was to ascend to love
to be loved, to see love
to feel love, to live love, to receive love
from my Adam, be his Eve
and make a wholesome life for me and he
but I give up and accept that that kind of love
will never dwell in my presence

This life

It all be over soon,
the broken promises, empty covenants and countless
disappointments
won't matter anymore
I will return safely home
back in the arms of my Father.

It will all be over soon,
the tears
I've cried through the years
will water my grave.

It will all be over soon,
and the desires this earthen vessel desired
will be retired.

It will all be over soon,
I will no longer surround myself
with the cares of this world
the pleasures of this place
won't be enough to keep me bound.

It will all be over soon,
I will be able to see
those who went on before me
I will be greeted by my creator
and wave goodbye to this side of life,
it will all be over soon
it will all be over soon

Minor chords

Tell me sister; what it is thus hath to speak?
for a while, oh but for a while doth we have to entertain
on this plain earth of a million degrees to somewhere.
Hopefully a place where we both can find unlocked doors
and treasures galore
so again I say, what is it thus hath to speak?

No laughing matter

It's funny how we easily forget growth and we quickly
eliminate people from our life.
It's funny how we easily discard relationships, ones that
greatly mattered days ago.
It's funny how we limit our hearts and stop the possibility of
healing.
It's funny how we waste time lying to ourselves, slurping a lie.
It's funny how we kill each other's dreams because we don't
have our own.
It's funny how we destroy sacred treasures, how we denounce
their value.
It's funny how we beg for more this or that and can't manage
what we already have.
It's funny how we ask for another chance when we know in
our heart that we didn't give our best the first time and the
only reason we're asking for a second chance is our ego.
It's funny how what we desire we really fear.
It's funny how we try to ignore the inner conflict going on
inside, how we try to appear normal;
who defined normality? Just wondering cause
I find it funny that we judge each other on frivolous facts,
and how we ask for forgiveness but don't forgive each other.

Who am I?

I am the lady that sings the blues
I am the woman who bears a Cross like Langston Hughes
I am the girl that die like the Alabama four
I am Maya's caged bird that wants to soar
I am the lineage of Black Moses,
the untold stories of Jim Crow
I am the dream of Martin Luther King,
do you hear the freedom bell ring
I am Nina Simone's b-flat
I am Jackie Robinson's 138th home run
I am read of in Fredrick Douglas' The Columbian Orator
I am a black woman, a single mother, with a thorn in her flesh
I am Sojourner Truth's "Ain't I a Woman Speech"
I am a great American poet

Every creation is God's
expression of love

A beautiful thing

Full of life, a love so liberally free
those looking at thee
may see a fool
but no fool are ye
understand there is a law working here,
the law of reciprocation
many don't get it how giving love gives gratification
the one you sprinkle it upon
may not be the one
to give it back
but it's coming back
love all creations
for when we love others we,
in turn are loving ourselves
for every creation is God's expression of love.

Running for my life

Generations of curses carried in a web of lies
the breed of a new seed admired sunny skies
limitless skies of hope and glory
not weathered for their hypocritical story
of pained yesterdays and hypnotic spells
spoken over the females
of our family
a black widow curse was embedded in our story
knowing something wasn't right
because all my life was a fight
a fight for love with all the wrong men
a fight for security in a sea of sin
my days were enthralled with confusion and distress
at thirty-five I sought wisdom from an enchantress
she confirmed what I already knew
many decades ago
the women in my family were plagued by voodoo
ready to be loosed, a solution was pursued
after receiving direction I humbly subdued
my soul rejoiced as I pictured my life free
free from loveless marriages, yes,
I was going to rewrite history
looking at the women in my family none were espoused did
neither did they aspire to be.
It was my heart's desire to experience love with a man
unconditionally
not only was there a curse needing a fix
there was a poor example of a man and father in the mix
without the desire to heal, these women didn't stand a chance
to heal, find love and experience true romance
it was clear what I wanted for my life
which was to meet my king and become his wife
believing with all my heart the solution I received

Running for my life (continued)

I bathed in salt water and opened my heart believing
I was free from the evilness done in our past
I thanked God profusely for a love that would last.
Shortly after this special ritual it became crystal clear
that my Boaz was always near
we wed nearly two years later
every day I see him, I thank my maker.
Generational curses are real and exist today
however there are solutions to make them go away
I ran for my life holding victory in sight
and no matter how tough it got, I did not give up the fight.

Starting over

I never thought I'd see the day when zeal would digress
I never thought I'd see the day when I dreamt no more.
I never thought I'd see the day when my belief in the power of
love would shift, that day is here and it frightens me.
I never thought I'd see the day where my first response was
not prayer.
I never thought I'd see the day when family was estranged.
I never thought I'd see the day where I had no vision for my
future.
I never thought I'd see the day of frugal hope,
that day is here and it frightens me.
I never thought I'd see the day where my mind travelled far
but the physical me sat still.
I never thought I'd see the day when I'd be insatiable.
I never thought I'd see the day where I'd lose interest in life.
I never thought I'd see the day life would crumble over and
over again.
I never thought I'd see the day I'd realize my strength and
stand firmly in it,
that day is here and it frightens me.
I never thought I'd see the day when it felt like answers were
far from me.
I never thought I'd see the day when my childlike demeanor
would resurface.
I never thought I'd see the day when I was no longer
fascinated by overcoming yesterday's challenges.
I never thought I'd see the day when I had no more fight
that day is here and it frightens me.

Is there one

I wonder what I could have done to be at this place,
this time and space
where I find myself feeling hopeless
the more I pray, the harder life seems.
I try my best not to get caught up in things
for the most part I do well
but today it's hard to tell
I'm provider for
even through breaths
I feel unsupported and alone
in a world all on my own
who do I tell my heartaches to
no one seems to listen long enough
everyone wants to give a solution
or judge my thoughts
find fault
but not listen long enough
to hear my heart's cry
or passing thoughts about how I want to die
how I feel lost in a world I once felt found
or that I feel bound
by thoughts of uncertainty
and ignominy.
Seems like the weapons are winning
this constant spinning in my head,
says I'm losing.

Looking for hope

The day came when time stopped,
time stopped in the rhythm of the night
the fight of the young, became the struggle of the old.

Soundtrack to life

Blowing in the frail wind of life passing by
I cry to the wind to free these distorted views
and everyday blues
that greet me
that cheat me
that beat me.

I want to hide from everyone and everything
my dreams, desires and hopeful plans
over the years have slipped through my hands.

Following a tune most people don't hear
it gets a little lonely out here.

Crying only blurs my vision
making it hard to breathe
thank God for the comforting angels
he sends to me.

Wandering in the listless beat of life slowed me down,
I sway to the indistinct tune of a distant reality
and emotional frugality
that taunt me
that daunt me
that haunt me.

Afraid to leap

Have you ever doubted what you see,
what you hear?
Have you ever doubted yourself?
even though you knew the truth
you doubted it, have you ever doubted truth
made truth to be a lie
looking to the clouds, they seem so full of doubt,
the weeping willow confirms my truthful resolutions
yet not believing them is not as easy as doubting peace
doubting the melodic song of the raven proves solace
Have you ever doubted yourself?
as the stream flows by the bay
so does doubting thoughts on the banks of my heart
questions, fear, and comfort washed away when spring
showers berated sunny days
have you ever doubted what you once believed?
what will it take?
touching the holes?
confirmation through souls?
what route should be taken to rid my shaken heart ?

With open arms

If it were only that easy
I'd click my heels, spin and make a wish
I'd sprinkle fairy dust and chant your name
I'd pluck a lock of your hair
I'd drink love's secret potion
but falling in love is more than a notion
so many walls to breakdown
so many fears to overcome
so many pains to release
so many truths to learn
so many lessons to study
so many ways to understand
so many adaptations
falling in love shouldn't hurt
falling in love shouldn't be scary, but it is
we shouldn't fall in love, but
let love fall upon us,
let love flow from us.

Wounds in the way

I can't pretend anymore, I won't
my heart longs to know yours
to open the closed doors of possibility.
I've never felt so strongly
that I was created for you and you were created for me
I want to know your rhythm,
you don't have to be afraid
I would never hurt you intentionally
let me be your student of love and learn your anatomy
I don't live on fantasy island
I know lasting love requires work
I'm willing to do my part
trust me,
trust me with your heart.

Too much time

So many times I wanted to call you
to clear the air
to get to the bottom of your truth.
Our friendship wasn't the best
but it outlasted the rest
can't believe it has been almost two years
since we have spoken or seen each other
with life being so short
I never thought this spat would last so long
though at times I often wished you could have been
a little deeper with the advice you gave
I'd give anything to catch up and shoot the breeze
to hear what set you off, clear the air, reconcile.
Our time a part was needed for growth
I'm sure life has changed for us both
how I never thought it would end
maybe suspend, but not end.
If our paths should be meet,
I pray it's not in the judgment seat
farewell my childhood pal.

Cynthia's song

Who can heal this broken heart
tattered by forsaken dreams,
torment hid in the offing of zeal
while trying to appeal
to a better way.

Who can mend this broken heart
where abandoned hope settled deep
inside the crevices of prosperity,
disparity,
dampened my ability
to know a love
that would bring me home.

Who can touch this demented heart
sanctioned with doubt
the promise of tomorrow
drowned in yesterday's sorrow
the deceitful brim
resist intimacy
remaining lost forever.

Who can find this bemused heart
for it longs to be found .

Abba father

It's going down, yesterday's prayers are coming to light.
I beseeched the throne for divine connections and rich
opportunities,
now that they are here
I am grappled with fear.
I will finish strong, keep going butterfly
I reaffirm at night looking at starry skies,
when perplexed cries
immobilize me,
praying fervently
seems as though it ain't doing the job,
I cry Abba Father, for I know my father will never forsake me.
I cry tonight, with a loud voice, Abba Father.

When I get close to the end
I tend to fall short.
Completion is in sight
yet I tend to fight
against myself
there is no one else
stopping or blocking me.

Abba father, I come to your thrown of grace
asking that you move me from this space
of doubt, unworthiness and uncertainty
for I know in my heart you have ordained this beauty for me.

You ordained my life, this path and my great ambitions
so I give my inner self permission
to be free,
and move oh so elegantly
in you.

Bit.ta.chon
Jeremiah 17:7

Upon rising
my wandering heart recalled night visions,
betraying pictures
proving to dishonor your vision, my Lord
consternation suspended the promise of peace straightway,
I prayed.

God calmed my simple heart
comforting words spoke he to me.
Come hither my child,
go, for thou art agile, resilient,
a promised vessel
with endless oil in thine possession;
designed to sanctify
timeless treasures,
and bless mankind benevolently.

Conversations with God

I wish I could have my wish come true
I wish I knew what to wish
I wish I knew if the desires of my heart were yours too God
I wish I knew your specific intentions for my life
I wish I knew how long it would be before you granted my
desire
I wish I knew if it would be worth the wait
I wish oh how I wish I knew the plans you have for my life
I wish I wasn't single
I wish I could walk on the riverfront with my husband
I wish he would give me his jacket if the chill was too cool
I wish he would learn me and love me as I am
I wish I could share all the love I have in my heart with him
I wish I could sing to him when he was sad
I wish I could encourage him when he felt low
I wish we could travel to places, exotic places
I wish we could go to an NBA game and eat popcorn together
I wish he would surprise me with special things
I wish I knew your plans God
I wish I didn't wish so much
I wish I could be content with the way things are
I wish I knew more

Keep me Father

Keep me Father, keep my foot from falling.
I stumble on my path and lose my way often.
I hear your voice but still stray at times
but no matter how it may seem,
I want to be kept.
You promised me
you'd never leave nor forsake me.
Sometimes I wonder though, feels like life try and break me.
I know the old cliché,
you would never give us more than we can bear,
but Lord the heaviness of my portion
is ripping a tear,
in the fullness of my faith.

Keep me Father,
keep my flesh for rising up and taking control
I get confused
because these desires
that you've infused
are part of my human makeup.
I try not to desire his touch without the ring
because even the thought is sin
seems like the battle I'm in
is with my flesh and my spirit
but the preacher say we in spiritual warfare
with the devil, I tend to disagree
seeing as how you've sacrificed yourself for me
and conquered the grave seeing how you walked perfectly
and never gave in to sin.

Keep me Father
keep my mind, keep my heart.

May

A sacred triumph mesmerized her gleeful heart
panting, breathing toxicity.
Why do things have to be so difficult,
asked she the wind.
The chill of the wind
bared no response for her longing soul,
mocked by the stars,
the moon tickled her curiosity
offering nothing.
Beckoning to know more,
the sun refused to appear
As the sky rolled over.

Pillow talk

Hey Father, I thank you for this day
even though things seem aloof
and my thoughts have strayed.
I pray to you cause that's what I've been taught,
to give thanks but I must say
I feel like I've been blindsided
misguided
like I've been bamboozled and yes, even hoodwinked
cause this uncertainty I think
has really gotten to me.

Under midnight skies
bellow I soul wrenching cries
cause Lord I can't quite seem to comprehend
your state of mind or the position I'm currently in.
See Lord, my heart really aches,
and I don't know how
much more of this I can continue to take.
I feel lost like I'm in a strange place
yes, Psalms 23 is very real to me
but I can't seem to quite comprehend
what kind of battle I'm in
so like David I pray that you teach my hands to war
but I'm exhausted from this fight
and these sleepless nights
are having their way with me.

God can I be honest, can I tell you the truth right now
I'm mad, I'm sad because all the dreams
that once seem to reverberate in my head
are no longer my friends and I can't seem to comprehend
how to play this game called life.
People say "don't question God,
Chile don't you know no better."

Pillow talk (continued)

but I say
if Jesus is the way,
the truth and the light
then surely I have a right
to ask for direction,
Them silly saints.

I'm tired God
I don't want to talk no more, don't want to listen either

Can I go to sleep now?

Prayers in the night

Gambling my soul, a covenant is formed
all the while I wonder will my dreams be harmed
rivers of love to flow through my veins
radiant skies of sunshine and rain,
rain to wash my sins away,
rain to cleanse me
to sanctify my sin sick soul from iniquity.
Tender mercies submerge this vessel of doom
deliver me from this impulsive flesh and,
send my groom.

Spirits

I feel them,
the ghosts
they watch me
they talk to me
they tell me how to succeed
they watch me cry
they laugh at me
cause they figure I ain't got a clue
they tell me to pray.

The ghosts, my ancestors
their wrenched attire
they watch me maneuver about,
and when I go to bed
they wait for me
to talk to them,
but I tell em
I don't feel much like talking.
they seem sad,
but I go to sleep
While they wait.

It won't matter

Arms folded, we retreat to our previous stance
prior to marriage it was clear we could make it on our own
but here we were building a life and home
yet finding trouble, stiff unwilling to bend
silently thinking to myself, will this matter at the end
when words cannot be heard, hugs no longer able to be given
will it matter when condolences are in order
will it matter when dirt become the final resting place.
What is there to lose here but pride
a destructive adversary that never really gets anyone anywhere
my anger is real, my pain is true
m dislike for disregard is genuine
but so is my need to move past this
because in the end it won't matter.

Broken wings

Acceleration inhibited, can't seem to fly right
crooked aim, can't seem to release the fight.
Conflicted because of who I am and who I've portrayed
a critical antonym,
a paradoxical mystery
wanting to free her story
unable to find someone to listen intently.
A diverse retrograde,
stifled and stuck in a grievous cage.
Difficult and annoyed, agreeing to be compatible
my heart lives to fly high in the sky
rummaging the low parts is where my soul remained.

These broken wings stifled my flight
appearing normal, a smile and humble stance fools them all.
This, far from a free fall,
unable to take flight, resting upon my shoulders,
a despicable sight.
Loomed vision, keeps me from soaring high,
or is it my unwillingness to be free,
my opposition to releasing this treachery.
Deceit have I hid in my heart.
dramatically opposed to speaking the messages of my heart
there has to be a place to release
here, here is where freedom reigns.
Yet even here, in this sacred place, holding back
seems to be the natural order,
this ruined soul has no home.

Pieces of me

Sitting at the lake admiring ripples from the wind
fascinated by harmony and flow, admiring how
separation hides her face.
The lines, free from abandonment, part of the whole.
A truth my soul finds hard to agree with.
The waves go into the sand trusting to be received,
how can I rid myself of this lonesome plague,
a terminal illness eating at the strands of my peace.
Disconnection, settles in like the sand welcomes the waves.
There, a peace union is made,
yet in my heart, fear of desertion riddles me
making it discomforting
when close to another.
Wearing myself thin
by maintaining this war I'm in.
I convince my mind it is not safe, getting close to another
the clouds laugh; I see their reflection on the lake.
They mock my sense of dereliction
promising it is merely my imagination.
The lake offers a question,
if we're all connected how can you fear being abandoned?
Pitifully I examine this body of water
eagerly dismissing the question.
After careful meditation I now understand,
it's not all of me that feels lost and alone
just pieces of me.

Buying time

Nothing here makes me want to stay
well maybe the two of them, but in some sadistic kind of way
taking them with me soothes my mind.
The products this world has for sale
does not appeal to my kind.
So while I remain, I buy time.
Daring greatly inviting dreamers to take part,
working lightly to open their hearts and.
scribing melodically.
My pen, matrimony, vowing to conjugate sanity and wit.
Reaching back, supporting sisters that mirror me
those residing in a place I've visited frequently.
Depression, confusion, feeling completely misplaced,
wanting to be free but unsure, it's written all on their face.
Seeing through to her soul, we journey together to better
places, immaculate spaces.
Second time around without a lead
Back and forth, my thoughts travel the beat on a swinging
clock
my love, nothing to question
this role of bride requires attention from the seat of my soul
like caring for a newborn babe, there is so much to know.
A journey to the center, reveals a score of crime
so for now, I go in peace and buy time.

God's eye

A troubled heart, life had taken a wicked turn
in the blink of an eye, life had served mockery.
Prayers beseeched decades before, opened the door
to a wretched path.
Lying one night, no hope for rest
my heart, heavy with concern.
Looking at the black sky wondering if recovery
was on the other side.
Vexed, my soul was vexed,
words of comfort lost direction
unable to locate my heart.
Sometime, after lying there, drifted into a deep sleep
the earth rotated slowly
placing God's eye directly before me.
Safe with me you are, the moon assured
as it illuminated my face.
The moon celebrated my existence.
it proclaimed excellence and howled
jubilee! Sweet jubilee
God came for me.
Seeing deep in my soul, the moon glorified
deep-seated fears of being left alone
persuading my locked heart to believe
God would never leave me.

Without words

While speaking, it was clear I couldn't buy her a clue
dumbfounded, she looked on, believing she knew.
What she knew was far from truth
stripping them of confidence
it was no coincidence
that her heart wouldn't allow her to see
her selfish ways.
Who can feet all those soles?
Looking behind their closed doors
would reveal their need for your excess
but inquire thee not.
a loss for words, amazed at the stinginess sitting on your back
you observe lack
not of strangers but those in your blood line
yet offering no support or care
unless something for you is in there.
I get speechless watching you
with a closed mouth, my heart utters words of hurt
not wanting to believe a being could be so greedy
and needy
at the same time.
Covering my mouth, holding back the tears
figuring what to do with the silence of years,
surely you can't be that ignorant
maybe you are.
How do you ignore your own
but go all out for those that freely come and go?
the definition offer you of love, perplexes me.
So, without interrogating, quietly sitting by
uttering no words, no conversation, only prayer.
Only prayer.

Small spaces

There's no room for my mind to breathe
no territory to call my own.
Cramped by the shortage of latitude,
I become unsettled.
Like a leaf blowing in the wind not cursed by limitation
I want to go free, I want to go far.
I want to soar on eagle's wings
ascending with great joy, sailing with colossal courage.
I want to travel long, journeying to places trepidation denied.
These confined parts are enmity to my future.
Ridding defeat's melody, my heart learned by default,
I grab audacity and fortitude,
holding them to the light, it's apparent,
more accessories are needed.
Looking up, I see grit, spirit and humor.
Smiling, they are loaded with the others.
To fly free, there can't be anything weighing me.
With outstretched hands, crucifying fear
driving stakes into small spaces,
taking flight and securing the sky
I arise to high places
where borders exist no more.

Cross over

The trance offered several hints, opening the canal
for truth to breathe.
In the distance, a bridge,
breaking away from a warped city,
a vulgar odor insulted lies told I the little girl inside
she believed it was safe where she was born to dwell.
He came to me, in the raggedy home childhood memories
were conceived.
His spirit was familiar however he was a stranger to me.
Assuring freedom from generations of agony,
affliction forefathers bestowed through ignorance and
uncivilized existence.
Standing in the room of great release, he invited me to lay
down my burdens
and come with him.
I had a choice to make,
I believed his heart was for me
I believed he came from heaven to get me.
Relieving the need to interrogate freed my heart to go.
It was night when he returned,
travelling, I take the city in, acquitting death sentences.
Landing before the platform to freedom
I look my angel in the eyes, we crossed over together.
He came to save me a thousand years before,
he came to know my love once more.
Crossing over, the bridge vanishes
destroying any possibility of going back Abaddon,
rivers of tears melt the residue of my weary heart.

Last dance

At the foot of my bed, starring off into the light
my mind paints pictures of you,
a wave of consolation appeared, tickling my inner lust
to have my way with you.
Envisioning our spin,
taking it all in makes me grin
cause I imagine an even and just event
like the olden days
Isaac comes to mind
his dance, pleasurable though slightly tricky
his sons devoted their ear at his bed side while he danced.
I want to dance like David danced.
I want to dance like Dorcas
Leave Lazurus' death for a beckoning heart.
My heart is excited, beating faster at the thought of you.
A glorious celebration, a feast for kings and queens
honoring my legacy
I beg thee to dance with me.
Wretched and worn, this woeful soul
craves a final sway.
Allow me to accompany loved ones long gone,
release this flesh and grace your throne.

Out of it all

Gleaming, glowing like a woman with child
it was hard not to smile.
The promise, luminous, making the pathway clear
in this moment, I was all out of fear.
The seed, matured, prospering into a lovely garden
nourishing my body, fickleness had been pardoned.
I was fresh out of feeling sorry for myself
my faith was ripe,
victory was in season.

Green with glory, I was out of it all,
all the little white lies and big bushy tales,
out of grimy little secrets of days olden
that try to keep holding
destiny hostage.

Tilling the soil of my heart, discovering a regal rectitude
the seed planter assured a lovely harvest.
So I prepared for the great reward vowing to the heavens
there would be no more lament,
discarding mealy fruit made room for ecstasy.
Out of misery, out of suffering, out of despair
out of discomfort, out of hopelessness, out of it all.

Shower me

Restless, unable to secure comfortableness in my bed,
searching my head for clarity
I should have been searching my heart instead.
Thrashing crashes of thunder disturbed my rest
flashing lights lit the sky putting patience to a test.
As thoughts of mayhem scooted by
looking like Monday morning blues
I beseeched the Holy Spirit of what to do.
Go outside and let the rain baptize you
Go, stand with your head to the heavens and let me feed thee.
Standing at the patio for what seemed like eternity
I knew the water was cold and would chill me.
Feeling the warm nudge of an angel near by
I opened the door, stepped out and let my heart comply.
Spreading my arms and lifting my head heaven bound
the rain showers offered peace, security and safety.
The love of God baptized me
The Holy Spirit washed me,
rinsed away residue of hopelessness,
washed away despair,
cleaning me as I prayed this prayer:
"Lord I need thee,
show yourself strong and mighty.
Lord I need thee,
show yourself strong and mighty.
Tears mingled with rain drops
as my soul freed herself from fear and uncertainty.

Stinky dude

Sitting next to him, a sweaty smelly man
angry thinking, "Why didn't he just stand?"
Seems like he tossed and turned the whole train ride
and the sour stench attached to his flesh did not hide.
With every bump, jolt and whip around
the stench from his soiled clothes, my nose found.
I couldn't stand it anymore, I had to get up
I shifted in my seat so much
the rocking of the train coupled with his foulness made me
have to throw up.
Abruptly standing and assuming a position near the door
I was only two stops ahead of where I normally board
but what the hell, I sit all day
what harm could be done anyway.
Avoiding eye contact by playing with my phone
all the while thinking, I hope he bathe when he gets home.
The train stopped, the doors opened wide
as I deboarded, the fresh air outside
had a lovely beat
bobbing my head and rocking I thought "my nostrils are now
free".

Playground

The world is my playground and life is the maze with the prize
in the center.
It's amazing, we hurt ourselves on the playground, yet we get
back up for another twirl.
The merry-go-round of love makes our head spin.
Jumping off the monkey bars, frightening, like pursuing new
areas of life.
Looking through the sand of possibilities finding discarded
treasures,
tirelessly you run to and fro, jumping, climbing and crawling
only to anticipate doing it again when lying in bed at night.
Sometimes on the playground, segregated flocks don't mix
and there is always a bully, your ego, selling deceptive
intelligence,
saying things like you're weak and not worthy to play.
Yeah, the playground taught us how to play while teaching us
how to live,
how to share, have fun, compromise and protect ourselves.
We rest at night waiting for another chance to play hopscotch
or jump rope maybe basketball or marbles
with friends, relieving stress.
Yeah the playground, a foundation for lessons
funny I still play, just got a different playground.

Liar, liar

You say you want a lady
but keep chasing rats.
You say you want a family
but you act like one of them hoodlum cats.
Let's settle down and make a life,
you say this with a straight face,
but you stay out all night
looking for a good chase.
Where is your job,
why you always asking me for cash
why you always on the prowl
for the next girl to smash.
You're a lil boy in a grown man's body
old as dirt still trying to be a hottie
your game is whack, your playa card revoked
go sit your butt down somewhere before you get choked
you ain't ready for a woman like me
my independence threatens you
my education does too
you ain't ready or on my level.

Psalms 92

Lord,
you always bring me back
to the peacefulness inside of me
to the beautifulness of humility
you always bring me back
to having an open heart and still mind
to accepting things will be in their own time
when I stray
you have a way
of bringing me back
thank you Father universe for loving me so
and helping me grow,
my life is not my own
so I lift my voice and sing this song
of gratitude and praise
for your mercy and grace
and for bringing me back
to our secret place.
Amen

I see me

I searched high and low
to know
what I know now, me!
In smelly sheets,
banging in streets,
tongues that lie,
telling me what I wanted to hear
trying to keep away tears,
but the pipe busted
and bottled pain
rained.
I saw her standing there
wet, lost, longing, lingering
in a place that was no longer her home
she was scared to be on her own
but here she was.
Now budding and free, me!
Smiling from ear to ear,
at one point she didn't want to be here.
Safe now, renewed and renowned
fresh and whole
what the devil thought he stole
she got back.
Once was blind,
now I see
I see me!
I see me!

Weight loss

Permission to release, to be acquitted of manifested burdens,
gross conduct revealed oversized obstacles
making it unpleasant to move,
the thought of enjoying life yield a hollow whale like
disposition making it unattractive.
I give myself permission to discharge fears attached to cellular
membranes, causing robust expansion.
It is no longer necessary for me to keep them alive,
ingesting all things pure
unlocking heaven's door, and release
releasing the need to believe perfection is a destiny,
releasing the belief there is something wrong with me,
releasing the need to think love is not for my kind
releasing the desire to know the answers all the time
releasing the fear to be supported by loved ones
releasing anxious motives of constantly feeling undone
releasing the pain of sexual guilt
releasing unlovable feelings about the way my body is built
releasing their opinions about my life
releasing the need to defend why I'm his wife.
Nurture my soul, fill these empty places with love.
So bowing gracefully
embracing passion and zeal to build a life worth waking to
embracing unconditional love able to break through
embracing the inner knowing provision is mine by divine right
embracing the universe is for me so there's no need to fight
embracing my past, the good, bad and obsolete
embracing the truth, I am perfect, whole and complete.

Maybe

Who am I to be great among men
to serve humanity through riches galore?
Who am I to be prosperous in the city
spreading abundance abroad?
Who am I to be magnificent in the land
gifting my whole self to the world?
Could it be, I was created for this magnitude of living
and I fear the essence of who I am?
Maybe, just maybe

Empty rooms

Heat bounces freely, flowing wall to wall
voices travel long and far, with nowhere to fall.
The echo confirms this room lost its flavor decades ago.
This airy place, anticipating creative flow
to land here and set free the blandness attached
splash paint on the walls with floral decorum to match
give life to me,
define a befitting personality
welcoming guests has been my song of delight
to keep private exchanges and watch slumbering souls
throughout the night.
Give me voice, robust, strong, and filled with glee
open up my heart for all the world to see.
Once a hollow shell lacking love and finesse
now bright and bodacious receiving lovely guests,
cool blues compliment creamy white
peach fuzz with sheer draperies to host sunlight.
Cherish your empty rooms
always nurture and groom
your heart.

Deep breaths

I helplessly stand near watching her,
watching her fight for her life
life seems so fragile, she can't catch her breath
she can't breathe, how can I help her
how can I comfort her the way a mom should
I watch them work on her to keep her here,
here in this life, I want her to stay with me
praying in between breaths,
don't know what I would do if I lost my child.
Death is not near, my heart knows of its distance and
is comforted it has not visited us this early morning
I love her, we have a bond that is thick and unbreakable.
the paramedics carry us to the ER, the woman in the back
assures me my daughter is doing fine
I smile, taking deep breaths trying to get myself together
I was scared, praising God through each breaths,
I kiss my baby girl and we fall asleep
waiting to see the doctor.

Losing touch

Trying to make her beautiful, a graceful beauty
the world would receive
she denied me the pleasure of teaching her.
Fighting me with all her might
in my dreams, my attempts to beautify her, lost.
What world would she meet
going out in such an unbeautiful way
my heart worried for her.
One way in day light, another at night
who was I dealing with here
who was standing before me
I hadn't a clue.
my words seemed to offend her
I was losing her,
losing her fast.
A mother's heart wants to know her daughter is equipped for
the world to the best of her ability
I wanted this to be her story
but she was constantly slipping away
my strongest weapon and ally was to pray
every day I pray.

Twisted

Wanting to eat the forbidden fruit, she questions her sexuality,
wrestling with childhood bible lessons and matrimony,
wondering how to make sense of her body craving
the touch of a women,
mixed emotions about how to proceed
what to tell her seed
believing her soul was destined to hell.
Should she kiss and not tell?
Introduced to sensual touches of a woman at an early age
she longed to feel such passion again,
a passion she never could feel with the touch of her man.
Like Paul she wanted this thorn removed
she didn't know what to do
her mind was all twisted.

Sandy beach and thick dark clouds

God knows I love her, momma that is, I love my momma
she is wise and full of support
momma taught me about faith without using words
her life was a story of faith,
only sixteen when she gave birth to me,
gratitude encompasses my heart,
though a child herself, she didn't get rid of me
momma was a woman of few words but when she spoke
she shared great insight.
Momma's cooking carried my burdens away
love, peace and wisdom were her ingredients of choice
a prayer warrior and seer of other worlds
her prophetic dreams saved my sister's life.
I love my momma,
she taught me how to be a woman and a good mother
we had our share of fights and making up
some good laughs and hearty tears
through the years
life taught me how to be compassionate toward my mom
to see the little girl that resides within her
I love them both more
every day, I love her more than the day before.
A lioness, protecting my twins,
we're different yet miraculously alike.
She offers me peacefulness, her arms comfort my soul
I love my momma.

Wheel of Light

You came, uninvited, resting upon my shoulders
bringing large boulders
of contempt; guilt was your name
not too far behind was fault and shame.
I felt you all seven places
my tree of life
was dying,
dying slowing.
No matter how hard I tried to get rid of you
more thoughts surfaced
calling forth the need for light blue.
Stifling my creativity and minimizing the truth,
I had to let go of you
meditating, centering myself with red.
Moving to my heart, from my head
I hold unconditional love deep within.
One by one my inner castle is unlocked
and the mystic river of peace flows
resurrecting my tree
opening the powers inside of me.

A woman's heart

The question came several times before
guess I was too afraid to open that door
see I had tried matrimony previously
after it ended, my heart wasn't sure it was for me
though I had often fantasized about doing it again
so much had come up, so many fears,
so many uncertainties,
and no guarantees.
When I met him I knew he was special,
a real friend
however I often questioned within
if he and I could successfully blend
our lives, our homes and our individual way of doing things
I didn't believe in my heart we could, so I denied the ring
I beat around the bush when asked why
I didn't want to lie
and didn't know a nice way to say what I felt
always desiring to be pursued
my heart felt renewed
when he never gave up on us
so the last time he asked, I said yes
my decision, part love based but some fear,
fear no one else would want me
fear that if they knew my secrets they'd scurry away
fear that I might be missing a chance at real love
fear of what we would not become.
I say often I love him, convincing others, so I think
but the real doubter is me.

Torn

I see her meanness, we suffer at the hand of it
I use to blame myself
at once I believed divorcing her father ruined her heart,
it seemed so angry with the world.
How do I handle her anger
she can't face the world this way
the world will eat her up and spit her out.
We are her friends, the ones who love her
why does she want to hurt us,
why does she want to make us pay?
Seems like she does not want to be here with me
I have to fix it, I have to get inside her heart and mend it
but the truth is, that's God's job
ever since he came into our lives,
she placed me behind enemy lines
am I not supposed to have a love life,
am I supposed to put my life on hold?
She demands what she does not give
in her heart, tolerance does not live
I can't yell at her all the time,
I have to teach her a better way,
she is a beautiful girl
that need to realize her enemy is not the world.

Thin walls

My heart sank,
the way he yelled I thought he was talking to a dog
awakened out of my sleep
to anger skin deep
belittling innocent hearts
someone should beat the crap out of him
for scaring the life out of that child
children should be taught,
not berated and made to feel small.
tears dropped as I silently prayed
for this grown man to leave this helpless child alone
a child that will still suffer, even when he is grown.
Ignorance is a curse, I wonder
who yelled at him this way, who made him feel small,
who showed him his feelings were not important,
who taught him to treat his wife and kids this way
his wife, no better.
Her profane and perverted tongue
whips the children, just for being kids
nothing in particular they did
how can you treat the one you carried in your womb
like a dog, like scum of the earth
she punished them for talking during her movie
made them kneel,
I heard the littlest one squeal
my heart dipped, I prayed for them and her heart,
shortly afterward they were freed
but not free.

Steps

Gradually climbing, humbly acknowledging
the need to take this route
though travelled many times before
in order to open the door of my heart
I must forgive.
Steep as it seems
watching mental pictures on reams
recalling tragedies that weighed me down
making elevation a drag.
Each step strengthens courage to let go and fully embrace
the life I chose to live
a life that chose me before time.
A life promise, no matter how steep the climb
empowered by God and with angels at my side
I will make it to the top.

Rise to greatness

Sometimes I wonder what is the purpose of my existence,
at times I feel a strong urge, a calling to greatness
but when I sit and think, trying to define greatness
I realize no definition offers itself to me.
At one point, I believed greatness was doing a huge deed
something that restored or saved mankind
but as time prevailed, greatness became mothering my
children
in a loving, safe and gentle environment
as the girls grew, greatness then became being all of me
expressing myself creatively
getting to know the real me
and in doing so, I realized
I was living beneath the abundant line
God said was mine.
So I opened my heart to living my full potential,
daring to dream, pouring my time and passion in my new child
greatness became building her to be strong and benevolent
and never giving up on the vision of seeing her thrive
Now as I look at my life, trying to balance it all
greatness has become not losing my mind
there are so many components to my life,
sometimes I feel I can't keep up.
So now greatness is giving up the need to control
greatness is learning to fly free and go with the flow.

Loving him

It's not about who is right or wrong
at the end and beginning of the day, I love him.
He makes me smile and trust me with his secrets.
For a long time, I was unsure of what love looked like,
learning to pay attention so close
learning to share my heart's concerns
freed me to easily love him,
he looks at me and inquire about my thoughts
before answering, before sharing the deepest parts of me
immediately I'm questioning
if it's safe to share
is it safe to be bare
yeah, we've made love before, cried in each other's arms too
but when it comes to sharing my thoughts I fear being judged,
or misunderstood
I wonder will he do that thing men do,
you know, offer solutions
when a woman just wants to be heard.
Sharing the dialogues in my head, he takes it all in
I feel relief coming from him,
he feels closer to me
I feel closer to him,
especially since he does not question my thoughts or offer
unsolicited advice.
When we argue or have that unspoken distance
he often says I'm just like him,
hard exterior but soft in the middle,
I declare I am nothing like him because he is stubborn,
he gently moves me to the mirror, standing behind me
he says we are one, you're stubborn too.

BV

Simply put, I hate you!
Who gave you permission to be here?
Who gave you permission to make my life uncomfortable?
I hate the stench you deposit; marking me
I hate the itch from your drip
leaving me feeling unclean,
I hate the imbalance you bring.
Where do you come from, why are you here?
What greater issue are you a symptom of?
What is your purpose?
Sexual guilt. Sexual guilt?
I can see how that can be so
but you know,
I have forgiven myself time and time again
and I will do it again and again
I forgive myself for laying with men I really didn't know
I forgive myself for the self-love I never really did show.
I invite you to leave body
you serve no purpose being here
and just so we're clear
you are not welcomed back.
Releasing the need to punish myself
I am forgiven of all sexual sins and regrets
You are free to leave my body and never return
you are free to return to your native land of lies,
untruths and deceptive intelligence.
I am healed, whole and forgiven
I am free from your grip, I am now living.

Dark night of the soul

Rising quickly, sitting on the side of my bed
it's 3:40 am and I am angry
I realize I am angry with him all over again,
making every other him pay.
Every place I turned I see him
I see abandonment again
when my daughter's father remarried and no longer had time
for their calls, they were no longer a priority in his life.
I relived his abandonment watching emotional distance
grow between my step-son and his father
though they reside in the same home
he abandons me again when he doesn't ask about his day
or when he don't make sure he ate,
or make sure he is prepared for tomorrow.
I felt the sting of abandonment when he wanted to beat her
instead of understand her,
her mother is a dope head
and her dad is angry with her grandmother
yet the little girl suffers.
I felt the heat of abandonment when he stopped calling
only six, she unaware of her mother's doing
filing child support
kept this girl apart
from her father,
though she played no role
and did not know what was going on
she lost her dad.
I want my heart free from this pain
God show me the way to release my anger.

Life path

A journey of self-discovery,
clearing the way for a heart full of trust.
Working through issues of trust, using faith to champion
the qualms of day to day living.
A passionate soul, whose first love is family,
and bringing beauty to the world.
An expressive empath, on a fast track,
moving forward without sometimes looking back.
Greatness is in my hands, if focus remains in my heart.
A teacher who never falls short
of the mystical teachings sent to teach
a light worker, embalmed in Spirit, destined to reach
imprisoned minds and lost souls.
Centering my mind through meditation and silence
connecting with Source,
often struggling with inner conflict
when drastically overtaken it can restrict
mobility, holding me hostage
thoughts of defeat and uncertainty
often get the best of me.
Life is a circle, complete and in full swing
my heart and soul is open
trusting my instincts, a fight
yet I war strong
all day long.

Home

It had been almost two years since seeing you
though I saw you every other night in my dreams
physically, our worlds were miles apart.
I didn't know what to expect the day we reunited
I could tell you missed me though
seemed like everywhere I went you were there.
A mutual meeting place brought us back together
it seemed like forever since I'd been home.
Our friendship was home,
it gave me peace and a place to retreat
when the concerns of living were weighing on me.
You, never one for too many words
but me, wordy and expressive,
without hesitation, told you how I missed you.
Though you didn't respond I felt your heart
I wanted to settle the matter
and get a fresh start
but it seemed like words were not the call of the day
my heart said to just let things fall as they may.
You invited me over, just like old times
sitting around the table, talking about life and sipping wine
I was home, back in my hood
I was with my childhood homies,
home, where I was welcomed and understood.
When I think about how things went
about why I was so bent,
I realized I wanted more for you
but had to be cool
with how you lived your life.
We don't talk every day and that's okay
I'm just glad to be home.

Happy times

Though far away, never forgotten
remembering when going up and down the aisle
supplying their needs
with ease
remembering when times we'd order in
and cuddle up watching television
remembering when my bed was bombarded
filled with six legs,
Saturday mornings, pancakes and sausage
on the patio.
Coming and going freely, money never a worry.
After we'd bond, over your dad's house you'd go
to give me a chance to clear my head and be alone.
I'd treat myself to a movie and dinner
then go to my favorite park,
sit by the waterfall at night
allowing my mind to fun free,
thinking about all the things I wanted to do with my life.
Happy times, welcoming them home
and helping them get ready for the week
playing dress up, sharing laughs and exchanging love.
Being a single mom does come with struggle,
trying to balance all the demands and have a life
but it comes with joy and a warm blanket of happiness
my daughters were safe, right at home with me.

Drama queen

She came twelve years under him
a little girl at heart
trying to tear apart
his bond with his seeds.
He, wanting to make things work this time
let her control the scene
tongue lash him in front of his kids
degrade him and shred his pride.
His children despised her,
they wanted daddy happy but not at the price he was paying.
What kind of woman tries to sever a father's relationship
with his children,
she was in competition.
I tried to talk to her, but he, her husband lied
somehow, he always was the victim
always declared he had no control.
Did he want it this way all along?
To erase his past by avoiding his children's calls
the last straw, when she fought my daughter
why couldn't people resolve issues
in a loving and respectable way?
Yelling and cussing, her response to everything
demands with hands across his face
she was a drama queen, the new misses.
We were from different worlds
hers, chaos and stupidity
She, his queen of drama
he, her dupe.

In the stillness

A cry for heaven opens my heart to the warmth of tomorrow.
Wavering and wallowing in truth of love,
freed me to go on in spite of my weary ways
the earlier days
when life made absolutely no sense.
In the stillness, my heart opens, shredding the need for pain
again and again,
thoughts of hope, that feeling, that moment when I realized
I will win, I was made to win, realizing
losing was not an option.
In the stillness my mind races
trying to find answers, the road map to sanity
soon I realized, sanity was there, right there in the stillness.
There was no need to look any further than my heart
all I needed was revealed in the stillness.

Wretched soul

It is time to go, my heart has left this place
wanting to erase
the day I said I do
the floor of my heart
bore a burden marriage could not heal
no longer wanting to conceal,
my inner truth, free me
I want to be free from matrimony
it is not how I pictured it to be.
I dream of death as an escape
a place where I can really lay down my burdens
without ridicule from anyone or anything.
I don't like him
I don't like his ways
he is immature, selfish and a functioning illiterate
what was I thinking, what did I think of myself
to marry this mirror image of yesterday
smiling at him, thinking quietly how I want to leave
am I attracted to losers, men with no vision?
am I attracted to broke brothers with no life plan?
am I attracted to absent fathers with victim mentalities?
what in me believes I am worthy of only this?
A wretched soul I am.

Beliefs, behaviors, because

Marinating in her disdain for them,
a species of incompetent, good for nothing beings
adopting her thoughts,
loving them became a fight.
My bones, immersed in her anger
they were different, not as good as us
growing, my life became a mission to prove her wrong,
they weren't all bad
basted in toleration, accepting things she wouldn't
deemed weak, dumb and lazy.
Cursed and doomed, headed for destruction
because I wanted to love them and be loved by them.
My brain, seething with her fears and inability to open up
nearly four decades later dispensing scorn.
The root, an unholy ruler
a predecessor that modeled less than loving behavior
he, insatiable and wicked
having no thought but for himself
his desires trumped the off springs'
placing barriers between them
intensifying her beliefs and behaviors
because it's the only way she knows.

The walking dead

A sheer curtain, a bubble, a mist of make believe
a hiding place, cramped and swamped with lies
lies about how life was supposed to be
looking for this so called life, claiming to have arrived
when things were going great, material possession
not only accentuated the falseness of the world
I believed existed, but made it easy to live.

This bubble was sucking the life right out of me
my vision was jaded and what I believed mattered
were by-products of a greater desire.
Anxiously wondering what this life was really about
conforming was no longer an option
but what should be done about the questions,
all the questions that exist in my head
what appears real feels so counterfeit.

Waking from this trance, mindful of the seeds planted,
outwardly and inwardly nothing is free of powerful energy.
Waking from this trance, becoming aware of liberating truths
yet searching for the path, the path that will lead me home.
Waking from the trance, food has lost its savor
success has a different flavor,
a veil lifted, the sheer curtain removed
clearly seeing hypocrisies.
Come out of the trance
this life is not about burning bushes or nails in trees
it's about accepting the truth of your being,
opening your heart and receiving unconditional love,
our bodies will fade but our spirit runs on.

Rocky road ice cream and turtles

Making a quick stop before heading home,
did the cashier know what kind of week it had been
did she think pre-menstrual cravings bullied me?
Here I was the day before the Sabbath,
adhering to a moment of self-indulgence,
this wasn't about chocolately sweetness
it was about honoring the girl inside,
the girl whose desires seem to took a back seat to survival.
I had come a long way from emotional eating,
meditation and prayer was my peaceful retreat,
but this night I wanted something to savor.
Just a few days ago, a mental breakdown.
Why did my thirties have to be this darn hard,
entering in the third decade of life from a cage of depression.
Agony and anguish, I thought it would subside, it never did.
My thirties began my spiritual journey, an awakening
tearing down every lie my life was built upon.
These turtles were just as I remembered,
for a brief moment my mind escapes reality
as the perfect blend of chocolate, caramel and pecans
make love to my mouth.
It hits me, the other side of this is two and a half years away
trying to look on the bright side while scooping rocky road,
looking at how far I've come, because
this use to be an every two week thing.
You're stronger, wiser and diligent,
you're beautiful and way more courageous than before.
Proud in the moment, these realizations came before eating the
whole pint of ice cream and only after one bite size turtle
was I reminded who I have become as a result of this
amazing spiritual excursion.

Not quite

Crying my heart out in the roomy space
only brought to my awareness
I was not quite there, better, but not quite there.
Steamy tears fell from my eyes while interrogating him,
my enraged heart wanted to know how he could leave so easy,
how could he betray me,
take back words he had spoken so passionately.
In the heat of life, when two should bind closer
his response was to retreat to a space
that only had enough room for him.
My soul, devastated, mourning with disbelief
that he was leaving me.
Our fight the other night should not resort to this
it was daddy leaving all over again,
wasn't I good enough for him to stay and work things out
wasn't I good enough for him to push aside his youth and
father me.
A million times I had forgiven daddy
his name took up more pages of my forgiveness journal
through the years than anyone else,
yet as my husband and I discussed our future
I saw plainly, I am not quite healed.

The pool at Bethesda

The path to the healing waters were entrenched with traps,
mud patches, sinking sand and rain clouds.
Stumbling several times on this journey
landed me face first in the dirt with creepy crawling things
some crawling on their belly, others, eight legged,
with pockets of poison at the tale and sharp teeth.
All taking a stab at me on my way to the pool of Bethesda,
the healing grounds, the place where restoration was my right.
When travelling there by star light
I could hear roaming creatures scavenging about
afraid, but so afraid to stop,
I keep moving.
The journey, long, hard and often confusing
resting a bit, needing to regain my composure
something bit me, immobilized and afraid
crawling to the pool became my only option.
Moving slower, seeing things from a lowly place
cringing every time snakes slithered by,
screaming howling sounds were near.
The pool, my destination, offered me solace and clarity
not to mention tranquility and harmony,
getting there was my life's plot
nothing would deter me, nothing would hinder me.
The shore of Bethesda welcomed me, as it waved,
assuring the waters were safe to join.
Ascending face first feeling rejuvenating
the waters closed painful places, moisturized dry places and
hydrated desiccated places making me whole again.
The pool of Bethesda baptized me and
removed lifeless pieces of my being.
I am alive!

Single parents

True winners, real heroes, single parents are amazing
we unselfishly share ourselves with our children
single parents are beautiful, courageous and game changers.
Though we didn't conceive our babies on our own
we work through our emotions of unfairness.
You get a gold star,
even the parents that secretly dream of a life without their kids
even parents that occasionally doubt themselves
even parents that can't make all the school events but make it
to most
even the parents that can't buy designer clothes but make sure
your child has a home
even the parents that fall asleep when your kid is reading to
you
even the parents that need some me time and have to get a
sitter
You get a gold star!
You are a jewel and your child is lucky to have you,
your love is making a difference.

Father Universe/Mother Earth

It is with great pleasure that I pray for the person reading this.
I ask they be encouraged to pursue their dreams with vigor and
tenacity. I ask that when they look out into the world, they see
beauty, support, guidance and divine opportunities. I ask that
when they are weak or discouraged that something or someone
would lovingly remind them how special they are to you and
the world. I pray that they will learn to trust your never failing
presence in their life and affairs. Whatever they call you,
God, Allah, Buddha, or Eloim it is my heartfelt prayer that
they allow you to increase their life in immeasurable ways.
I pray for harmony within so it can be expressed without. I
touch and agree with them regarding their
dreams/visions/goals that they come to pass according to your
will; align them with their highest good and always direct their
paths.

Amen.   Ashe.   And so it is.

String of pearls

Yoked about, wondering carefully
how closely do I resemble your enemy?
feel like you're just visiting here
with a hidden agenda
to destroy or rebuild.

Choked in an unknown tongue
seeking expression and to be understood
clearing my throat, taking a new approach.
In the heat of mid-year,
the seed was ripe and ready to pluck
a beautiful madam, created to touch the masses.

Cloaked in fear, full of what-ifs
forever looking for a sure thing
dying slowly for lack of nourishment
severing a hopeful end.

Soaked in the possibility of a happy ending
somehow always getting in the way,
never allowing it to naturally unfold,
too inquisitive for her own good.

Made in the USA
Columbia, SC
25 September 2019